GW00496737

Dedicated to
David, Lexi, Ash, Dina,

Gaby and Rivki Weinberg

My Little Black Doggy
is very *special*
to me

He has an *invisible illness* you can't see

sometimes
he's happy

sometimes
     he's sad

sometimes
he's cheeky

Sometimes
he's bad

My Little Black Doggy
is very *special*
to me

He has an
invisible illness
you can't see

Zzzzz

Sometimes
he sleeps

Sometimes
he doesn't eat

I know it's not
my doggy
that's not ok

It's his depression
  that rules the way

It's ok
   my doggy
      loves me always

he has a
special bark
that's unlike
any other dog
in the world

Lauren Posner

Lauren Posner is a Social Media
and Marketing Specialist
and author of My Little Black Doggy.

Lauren has spent a number of years researching and blogging about
mental health and 'Invisible Illnesses'. After having experienced it
within her family. In 2018 Lauren started the project 'I am visible'
an educational website giving a voice to people with Invisible
Illnesses. Her latest work is a series of children's mental health
picture books, educating children on invisible illnesses.

Martyn Niman

Martyn Niman runs animation studio King Bee (KingBee.co.uk) & illustrator of My Little Black Dog.

The characters in this book are based on real life characters.

Having experienced mental health within my close family I saw it was difficult for young children to understand what it means for a parent or adult to have depression with their parental behaviour being limited or different as a result of this.

Being unwell as a 5+ year old meant 'daddy's sleeping, so daddy is not feeling well again'... It was painful to see a child not understanding that daddy was unable to be daddy at that time and that daddy didn't love them any less. Symptoms of depression were just being displayed.

Depression is also referred to as 'The Black Dog'.

Lexi, our Cockerpoo puppy, was a lifeline to our family, and she inspired me to write a children's mental health picture book based on the signs of depression.

Lexi represents the adult with depression, expressed through 'my little black doggy', in the form of emotions and behaviour. The boy in the story is based on my eldest stepson Ash.

I wrote this story to help children understand the signs of depression from a young age and to be reassured that they are not to blame. Mental health is the cause and they are still loved.

Printed in Poland
by Amazon Fulfillment
Poland Sp. z o.o., Wrocław